This Audition Notebook Belongs to:

....

Production _____   Date _____

Role _____   Time _____

Casting Director _____   Location _____

Sides ☐   Headshot ☐   Resume ☐

Pieces Performed

1. _____
2. _____
3. _____

Outfit _____

Behind the Table

Name	Contact Info	Feedback Received

Notes

_____

Feeling   Call Back? ☐

Production _____   Date _____

Role _____   Time _____

Casting Director _____   Location _____

Sides ☐   Headshot ☐   Resume ☐

Pieces Performed

1. _____
2. _____
3. _____

Outfit _____

Behind the Table

Name	Contact Info	Feedback Received

Notes

Feeling   Call Back? ☐

Production _____   Date _____

Role _____   Time _____

Casting Director _____   Location _____

Sides ☐   Headshot ☐   Resume ☐

Pieces Performed

1. _____
2. _____
3. _____

Outfit _____

Behind the Table

Name	Contact Info	Feedback Received

Notes

_____

Feeling   Call Back? ☐

Production _____   Date _____

Role _____   Time _____

Casting Director _____ Location _____

Sides ☐   Headshot ☐   Resume ☐

Pieces Performed

1. _____
2. _____
3. _____

Outfit _____

Behind the Table

Name	Contact Info	Feedback Received

Notes

_____
_____
_____
_____

Feeling   Call Back? ☐

Production _____   Date _____

Role _____   Time _____

Casting Director _____   Location _____

Sides ☐   Headshot ☐   Resume ☐

Pieces Performed

1. _____
2. _____
3. _____

Outfit _____

Behind the Table

Name	Contact Info	Feedback Received

Notes

_____

Feeling   Call Back? ☐

Production _____   Date _____

Role _____   Time _____

Casting Director _____   Location _____

Sides ☐   Headshot ☐   Resume ☐

Pieces Performed

1. _____
2. _____
3. _____

Outfit _____

Behind the Table

Name	Contact Info	Feedback Received

Notes

Feeling   Call Back? ☐

Production _____   Date _____

Role _____   Time _____

Casting Director _____   Location _____

Sides ☐   Headshot ☐   Resume ☐

Pieces Performed

1. _____
2. _____
3. _____

Outfit _____

Behind the Table

Name	Contact Info	Feedback Received

Notes

Feeling   Call Back? ☐

Production _____   Date _____

Role _____   Time _____

Casting Director _____   Location _____

Sides ☐   Headshot ☐   Resume ☐

Pieces Performed

1. _____
2. _____
3. _____

Outfit _____

Behind the Table

Name	Contact Info	Feedback Received

Notes

Feeling    Call Back? ☐

Production _____   Date _____

Role _____   Time _____

Casting Director _____   Location _____

Sides ☐   Headshot ☐   Resume ☐

Pieces Performed

1. _____
2. _____
3. _____

Outfit _____

Behind the Table

Name	Contact Info	Feedback Received

Notes

Feeling   Call Back? ☐

Production _____   Date _____

Role _____   Time _____

Casting Director _____   Location _____

Sides ☐   Headshot ☐   Resume ☐

Pieces Performed

1. _____
2. _____
3. _____

Outfit _____

Behind the Table

Name	Contact Info	Feedback Received

Notes

_____

Feeling   Call Back? ☐

Production _____   Date _____

Role _____   Time _____

Casting Director _____   Location _____

Sides ☐   Headshot ☐   Resume ☐

Pieces Performed

1. _____
2. _____
3. _____

Outfit _____

Behind the Table

Name	Contact Info	Feedback Received

Notes

_____

Feeling   Call Back? ☐

Production _____   Date _____

Role _____   Time _____

Casting Director _____   Location _____

Sides ☐   Headshot ☐   Resume ☐

Pieces Performed

1. _____
2. _____
3. _____

Outfit _____

Behind the Table

Name	Contact Info	Feedback Received

Notes

_____

Feeling   Call Back? ☐

Production _____ Date _____

Role _____ Time _____

Casting Director _____ Location _____

Sides ☐   Headshot ☐   Resume ☐

Pieces Performed

1. _____
2. _____
3. _____

Outfit _____

Behind the Table

Name	Contact Info	Feedback Received

Notes

_____

Feeling    Call Back? ☐

Production _____   Date _____

Role _____   Time _____

Casting Director _____   Location _____

Sides ☐   Headshot ☐   Resume ☐

Pieces Performed

1. _____
2. _____
3. _____

Outfit _____

Behind the Table

Name	Contact Info	Feedback Received

Notes

Feeling   Call Back? ☐

Production _____ Date _____

Role _____ Time _____

Casting Director _____ Location _____

Sides ☐ Headshot ☐ Resume ☐

Pieces Performed

1. _____
2. _____
3. _____

Outfit _____

Behind the Table

Name	Contact Info	Feedback Received

Notes

Feeling   Call Back? ☐

Production _____   Date _____

Role _____   Time _____

Casting Director _____   Location _____

Sides ☐   Headshot ☐   Resume ☐

Pieces Performed

1. _____
2. _____
3. _____

Outfit _____

Behind the Table

Name	Contact Info	Feedback Received

Notes

Feeling   Call Back? ☐

Production _____   Date _____

Role _____   Time _____

Casting Director _____   Location _____

Sides ☐   Headshot ☐   Resume ☐

Pieces Performed

1. _____
2. _____
3. _____

Outfit _____

Behind the Table

Name	Contact Info	Feedback Received

Notes

Feeling   Call Back? ☐

Production _____   Date _____

Role _____   Time _____

Casting Director _____   Location _____

Sides ☐   Headshot ☐   Resume ☐

Pieces Performed

1. _____
2. _____
3. _____

Outfit _____

Behind the Table

Name	Contact Info	Feedback Received

Notes

Feeling    Call Back? ☐

Production _____   Date _____

Role _____   Time _____

Casting Director _____   Location _____

Sides ☐   Headshot ☐   Resume ☐

Pieces Performed

1. _____
2. _____
3. _____

Outfit _____

Behind the Table

Name	Contact Info	Feedback Received

Notes

Feeling   Call Back? ☐

Production _____ **Date** _____

Role _____ Time _____

Casting Director _____ Location _____

Sides ☐   Headshot ☐   Resume ☐

Pieces Performed

1. _____
2. _____
3. _____

Outfit _____

Behind the Table

Name	Contact Info	Feedback Received

Notes

_____

Feeling   Call Back? ☐

Production _____   Date _____

Role _____   Time _____

Casting Director _____   Location _____

Sides ☐   Headshot ☐   Resume ☐

Pieces Performed

1. _____
2. _____
3. _____

Outfit _____

Behind the Table

Name	Contact Info	Feedback Received

Notes

Feeling   Call Back? ☐

Production _____   Date _____

Role _____   Time _____

Casting Director _____   Location _____

Sides ☐   Headshot ☐   Resume ☐

Pieces Performed

1. _____

2. _____

3. _____

Outfit _____

Behind the Table

Name	Contact Info	Feedback Received

Notes

Feeling   😀   Call Back? ☐

Production _____ Date _____

Role _____ Time _____

Casting Director _____ Location _____

Sides ☐   Headshot ☐   Resume ☐

Pieces Performed

1. _____
2. _____
3. _____

Outfit _____

Behind the Table

Name	Contact Info	Feedback Received

Notes

_____

Feeling   Call Back? ☐

Production: _____   Date: _____

Role: _____   Time: _____

Casting Director: _____   Location: _____

Sides ☐   Headshot ☐   Resume ☐

Pieces Performed

1. _____
2. _____
3. _____

Outfit: _____

Behind the Table

Name	Contact Info	Feedback Received

Notes

Feeling   Call Back? ☐

Production _____   Date _____

Role _____   Time _____

Casting Director _____   Location _____

Sides ☐   Headshot ☐   Resume ☐

Pieces Performed

1. _____
2. _____
3. _____

Outfit _____

Behind the Table

Name	Contact Info	Feedback Received

Notes

_____

Feeling   Call Back? ☐

Production _____   Date _____

Role _____   Time _____

Casting Director _____   Location _____

Sides ☐   Headshot ☐   Resume ☐

Pieces Performed

1. _____
2. _____
3. _____

Outfit _____

Behind the Table

Name	Contact Info	Feedback Received

Notes

_____

Feeling   Call Back? ☐

Production _____ Date _____

Role _____ Time _____

Casting Director _____ Location _____

Sides ☐ Headshot ☐ Resume ☐

Pieces Performed

1. _____
2. _____
3. _____

Outfit _____

Behind the Table

Name	Contact Info	Feedback Received

Notes

Feeling   Call Back? ☐

Production _____ **Date** _____

Role _____ Time _____

Casting Director _____ Location _____

Sides ☐   Headshot ☐   Resume ☐

Pieces Performed

1. _____

2. _____

3. _____

Outfit _____

Behind the Table

Name	Contact Info	Feedback Received

Notes

[   ]

Feeling   Call Back? ☐

Production _____   Date _____

Role _____   Time _____

Casting Director _____   Location _____

Sides ☐   Headshot ☐   Resume ☐

Pieces Performed

1. _____

2. _____

3. _____

Outfit _____

Behind the Table

Name	Contact Info	Feedback Received

Notes

[   ]

Feeling   Call Back? ☐

Production _____ **Date** _____

Role _____ Time _____

Casting Director _____ Location _____

Sides ☐   Headshot ☐   Resume ☐

Pieces Performed

1. _____
2. _____
3. _____

Outfit _____

Behind the Table

Name	Contact Info	Feedback Received

Notes

Feeling   Call Back? ☐

Production _____ Date _____

Role _____ Time _____

Casting Director _____ Location _____

Sides ☐   Headshot ☐   Resume ☐

Pieces Performed

1. _____
2. _____
3. _____

Outfit _____

Behind the Table

Name	Contact Info	Feedback Received

Notes

_____

Feeling   Call Back? ☐

Production _____   Date _____

Role _____   Time _____

Casting Director _____   Location _____

Sides ☐   Headshot ☐   Resume ☐

Pieces Performed

1. _____
2. _____
3. _____

Outfit _____

Behind the Table

Name	Contact Info	Feedback Received

Notes

[   ]

Feeling   Call Back? ☐

Production	_____	Date	_____
Role	_____	Time	_____
Casting Director	_____	Location	_____

Sides ☐   Headshot ☐   Resume ☐

Pieces Performed

1. _____
2. _____
3. _____

Outfit _____

Behind the Table

Name	Contact Info	Feedback Received

Notes

Feeling 😕 😪 😮 🙂 😃   Call Back? ☐

Production _____   Date _____

Role _____   Time _____

Casting Director _____   Location _____

Sides ☐   Headshot ☐   Resume ☐

Pieces Performed

1. _____
2. _____
3. _____

Outfit _____

Behind the Table

Name	Contact Info	Feedback Received

Notes

Feeling   Call Back? ☐

Production _____ Date _____

Role _____ Time _____

Casting Director _____ Location _____

Sides ☐   Headshot ☐   Resume ☐

Pieces Performed

1. _____
2. _____
3. _____

Outfit _____

Behind the Table

Name	Contact Info	Feedback Received

Notes

_____

Feeling   Call Back? ☐

Production _____   Date _____

Role _____   Time _____

Casting Director _____   Location _____

Sides ☐   Headshot ☐   Resume ☐

Pieces Performed

1. _____
2. _____
3. _____

Outfit _____

Behind the Table

Name	Contact Info	Feedback Received

Notes

Feeling   😀   Call Back? ☐

Production: _____   Date: _____

Role: _____   Time: _____

Casting Director: _____   Location: _____

Sides ☐   Headshot ☐   Resume ☐

Pieces Performed

1. _____
2. _____
3. _____

Outfit: _____

Behind the Table

Name	Contact Info	Feedback Received

Notes

Feeling   Call Back? ☐

Production _____   Date _____

Role _____   Time _____

Casting Director _____   Location _____

Sides ☐   Headshot ☐   Resume ☐

Pieces Performed

1. _____
2. _____
3. _____

Outfit _____

Behind the Table

Name	Contact Info	Feedback Received

Notes

_____

Feeling   Call Back? ☐

Production _____   Date _____

Role _____   Time _____

Casting Director _____   Location _____

Sides ☐   Headshot ☐   Resume ☐

Pieces Performed

1. _____
2. _____
3. _____

Outfit _____

Behind the Table

Name	Contact Info	Feedback Received

Notes

_____

Feeling   Call Back? ☐

Production _____   Date _____

Role _____   Time _____

Casting Director _____ Location _____

Sides ☐   Headshot ☐   Resume ☐

Pieces Performed

1. _____
2. _____
3. _____

Outfit _____

Behind the Table

Name	Contact Info	Feedback Received

Notes

_____

Feeling   Call Back? ☐

Production _____   Date _____

Role _____   Time _____

Casting Director _____   Location _____

Sides ☐   Headshot ☐   Resume ☐

Pieces Performed

1. _____
2. _____
3. _____

Outfit _____

Behind the Table

Name	Contact Info	Feedback Received

Notes

_____

Feeling   Call Back? ☐

Production _____   Date _____

Role _____   Time _____

Casting Director _____   Location _____

Sides ☐   Headshot ☐   Resume ☐

Pieces Performed

1. _____

2. _____

3. _____

Outfit _____

Behind the Table

Name	Contact Info	Feedback Received

Notes

Feeling   Call Back? ☐

Production _____   Date _____

Role _____   Time _____

Casting Director _____   Location _____

Sides ☐   Headshot ☐   Resume ☐

Pieces Performed

1. _____

2. _____

3. _____

Outfit _____

Behind the Table

Name	Contact Info	Feedback Received

Notes

_____
_____
_____
_____

Feeling   Call Back? ☐

Production _____ **Date** _____

Role _____ Time _____

Casting Director _____ Location _____

Sides ☐   Headshot ☐   Resume ☐

Pieces Performed

1. _____
2. _____
3. _____

Outfit _____

Behind the Table

Name	Contact Info	Feedback Received

Notes

Feeling   Call Back? ☐

Production _____   Date _____

Role _____   Time _____

Casting Director _____   Location _____

Sides ☐   Headshot ☐   Resume ☐

Pieces Performed

1. _____
2. _____
3. _____

Outfit _____

Behind the Table

Name	Contact Info	Feedback Received

Notes

_____
_____
_____
_____

Feeling   Call Back? ☐

Production _____ **Date** _____

Role _____ Time _____

Casting Director _____ Location _____

Sides ☐   Headshot ☐   Resume ☐

Pieces Performed

1. _____
2. _____
3. _____

Outfit _____

Behind the Table

Name	Contact Info	Feedback Received

Notes

Feeling   Call Back? ☐

Production _____   Date _____

Role _____   Time _____

Casting Director _____   Location _____

Sides ☐   Headshot ☐   Resume ☐

Pieces Performed

1. _____
2. _____
3. _____

Outfit _____

Behind the Table

Name	Contact Info	Feedback Received

Notes

Feeling   Call Back? ☐

Production _____   Date _____

Role _____   Time _____

Casting Director _____   Location _____

Sides ☐   Headshot ☐   Resume ☐

Pieces Performed

1. _____
2. _____
3. _____

Outfit _____

Behind the Table

Name	Contact Info	Feedback Received

Notes

_____

Feeling   Call Back? ☐

Production _____   Date _____

Role _____   Time _____

Casting Director _____   Location _____

Sides ☐   Headshot ☐   Resume ☐

Pieces Performed

1. _____
2. _____
3. _____

Outfit _____

Behind the Table

Name	Contact Info	Feedback Received

Notes

Feeling   Call Back? ☐

Production _____   Date _____

Role _____   Time _____

Casting Director _____   Location _____

Sides ☐   Headshot ☐   Resume ☐

Pieces Performed

1. _____
2. _____
3. _____

Outfit _____

Behind the Table

Name	Contact Info	Feedback Received

Notes

Feeling   Call Back? ☐

Production _____   Date _____

Role _____   Time _____

Casting Director _____   Location _____

Sides ☐   Headshot ☐   Resume ☐

Pieces Performed

1. _____
2. _____
3. _____

Outfit _____

Behind the Table

Name	Contact Info	Feedback Received

Notes

Feeling   Call Back? ☐

Production _____   Date _____

Role _____   Time _____

Casting Director _____   Location _____

Sides ☐   Headshot ☐   Resume ☐

Pieces Performed

1. _____
2. _____
3. _____

Outfit _____

Behind the Table

Name	Contact Info	Feedback Received

Notes

Feeling   Call Back? ☐

Production _____ Date _____

Role _____ Time _____

Casting Director _____ Location _____

Sides ☐   Headshot ☐   Resume ☐

Pieces Performed

1. _____
2. _____
3. _____

Outfit _____

Behind the Table

Name	Contact Info	Feedback Received

Notes

Feeling 😕 😮 😲 🙂 😀   Call Back? ☐

Production _____   Date _____

Role _____   Time _____

Casting Director _____   Location _____

Sides ☐   Headshot ☐   Resume ☐

Pieces Performed

1. _____
2. _____
3. _____

Outfit _____

Behind the Table

Name	Contact Info	Feedback Received

Notes

Feeling   Call Back? ☐

Production _____   Date _____

Role _____   Time _____

Casting Director _____   Location _____

Sides ☐   Headshot ☐   Resume ☐

Pieces Performed

1. _____
2. _____
3. _____

Outfit _____

Behind the Table

Name	Contact Info	Feedback Received

Notes

_____

Feeling   Call Back? ☐

Production _____   Date _____

Role _____   Time _____

Casting Director _____   Location _____

Sides ☐   Headshot ☐   Resume ☐

Pieces Performed

1. _____
2. _____
3. _____

Outfit _____

Behind the Table

Name	Contact Info	Feedback Received

Notes

Feeling   Call Back? ☐

Production _____   **Date** _____

Role _____   Time _____

Casting Director _____   Location _____

Sides ☐   Headshot ☐   Resume ☐

Pieces Performed

1. _____
2. _____
3. _____

Outfit _____

Behind the Table

Name	Contact Info	Feedback Received

Notes

Feeling   Call Back? ☐

Production _____   Date _____

Role _____   Time _____

Casting Director _____   Location _____

Sides ☐   Headshot ☐   Resume ☐

Pieces Performed

1. _____

2. _____

3. _____

Outfit _____

Behind the Table

Name	Contact Info	Feedback Received

Notes

Feeling   Call Back? ☐

Production _____   Date _____

Role _____   Time _____

Casting Director _____   Location _____

Sides ☐   Headshot ☐   Resume ☐

Pieces Performed

1. _____
2. _____
3. _____

Outfit _____

Behind the Table

Name	Contact Info	Feedback Received

Notes

Feeling   😀   Call Back? ☐

Production _____   Date _____

Role _____   Time _____

Casting Director _____   Location _____

Sides ☐   Headshot ☐   Resume ☐

Pieces Performed

1. _____
2. _____
3. _____

Outfit _____

Behind the Table

Name	Contact Info	Feedback Received

Notes

Feeling   Call Back? ☐

Production _____   Date _____

Role _____   Time _____

Casting Director _____   Location _____

Sides ☐   Headshot ☐   Resume ☐

Pieces Performed

1. _____
2. _____
3. _____

Outfit _____

Behind the Table

Name	Contact Info	Feedback Received

Notes

Feeling   Call Back? ☐

Production _____   Date _____

Role _____   Time _____

Casting Director _____   Location _____

Sides ☐   Headshot ☐   Resume ☐

Pieces Performed

1. _____
2. _____
3. _____

Outfit _____

Behind the Table

Name	Contact Info	Feedback Received

Notes

Feeling   Call Back? ☐

Production _____   Date _____

Role _____   Time _____

Casting Director _____   Location _____

Sides ☐   Headshot ☐   Resume ☐

Pieces Performed

1. _____
2. _____
3. _____

Outfit _____

Behind the Table

Name	Contact Info	Feedback Received

Notes

Feeling 😐 😮 😲 🙂 😃   Call Back? ☐

Production _____   Date _____

Role _____   Time _____

Casting Director _____   Location _____

Sides ☐   Headshot ☐   Resume ☐

Pieces Performed

1. _____
2. _____
3. _____

Outfit _____

Behind the Table

Name	Contact Info	Feedback Received

Notes

_____

Feeling   Call Back? ☐

Production _____   Date _____

Role _____   Time _____

Casting Director _____   Location _____

Sides ☐   Headshot ☐   Resume ☐

Pieces Performed

1. _____
2. _____
3. _____

Outfit _____

Behind the Table

Name	Contact Info	Feedback Received

Notes

Feeling   Call Back? ☐

Production _____   Date _____

Role _____   Time _____

Casting Director _____   Location _____

Sides ☐   Headshot ☐   Resume ☐

Pieces Performed

1. _____
2. _____
3. _____

Outfit _____

Behind the Table

Name	Contact Info	Feedback Received

Notes

Feeling   Call Back? ☐

Production _____   Date _____

Role _____   Time _____

Casting Director _____   Location _____

Sides ☐   Headshot ☐   Resume ☐

Pieces Performed

1. _____
2. _____
3. _____

Outfit _____

Behind the Table

Name	Contact Info	Feedback Received

Notes

_____

Feeling 😐 😮 😲 🙂 😃   Call Back? ☐

Production _____   Date _____

Role _____   Time _____

Casting Director _____   Location _____

Sides ☐   Headshot ☐   Resume ☐

Pieces Performed

1. _____
2. _____
3. _____

Outfit _____

Behind the Table

Name	Contact Info	Feedback Received

Notes

Feeling   Call Back? ☐

Production _____   Date _____

Role _____   Time _____

Casting Director _____   Location _____

Sides ☐   Headshot ☐   Resume ☐

Pieces Performed

1. _____
2. _____
3. _____

Outfit _____

Behind the Table

Name	Contact Info	Feedback Received

Notes

Feeling   😃   Call Back? ☐

Production _____   Date _____

Role _____   Time _____

Casting Director _____   Location _____

Sides ☐   Headshot ☐   Resume ☐

Pieces Performed

1. _____
2. _____
3. _____

Outfit _____

Behind the Table

Name	Contact Info	Feedback Received

Notes

Feeling   Call Back? ☐

Production _____   Date _____

Role _____   Time _____

Casting Director _____   Location _____

Sides ☐   Headshot ☐   Resume ☐

Pieces Performed

1. _____
2. _____
3. _____

Outfit _____

Behind the Table

Name	Contact Info	Feedback Received

Notes

_____
_____
_____
_____

Feeling   Call Back? ☐

Production _____   Date _____

Role _____   Time _____

Casting Director _____   Location _____

Sides ☐   Headshot ☐   Resume ☐

Pieces Performed

1. _____
2. _____
3. _____

Outfit _____

Behind the Table

Name	Contact Info	Feedback Received

Notes

_____

Feeling   Call Back? ☐

Production _____ Date _____

Role _____ Time _____

Casting Director _____ Location _____

Sides ☐   Headshot ☐   Resume ☐

Pieces Performed

1. _____
2. _____
3. _____

Outfit _____

Behind the Table

Name	Contact Info	Feedback Received

Notes

Feeling 😐 😪 😮 🙂 😀   Call Back? ☐

Production _____ **Date** _____

Role _____ Time _____

Casting Director _____ Location _____

Sides ☐   Headshot ☐   Resume ☐

Pieces Performed

1. _____
2. _____
3. _____

Outfit _____

Behind the Table

Name	Contact Info	Feedback Received

Notes

Feeling    Call Back? ☐

Production _____   Date _____

Role _____   Time _____

Casting Director _____ Location _____

Sides ☐   Headshot ☐   Resume ☐

Pieces Performed

1. _____
2. _____
3. _____

Outfit _____

Behind the Table

Name	Contact Info	Feedback Received

Notes

Feeling    Call Back? ☐

Production _____   Date _____

Role _____   Time _____

Casting Director _____   Location _____

Sides ☐   Headshot ☐   Resume ☐

Pieces Performed

1. _____
2. _____
3. _____

Outfit _____

Behind the Table

Name	Contact Info	Feedback Received

Notes

Feeling   Call Back? ☐

Production _____   Date _____

Role _____   Time _____

Casting Director _____   Location _____

Sides ☐   Headshot ☐   Resume ☐

Pieces Performed

1. _____
2. _____
3. _____

Outfit _____

Behind the Table

Name	Contact Info	Feedback Received

Notes

Feeling    Call Back? ☐

Production _____ Date _____

Role _____ Time _____

Casting Director _____ Location _____

Sides ☐ Headshot ☐ Resume ☐

Pieces Performed

1. _____
2. _____
3. _____

Outfit _____

Behind the Table

Name	Contact Info	Feedback Received

Notes

Feeling   Call Back? ☐

Production _____   Date _____

Role _____   Time _____

Casting Director _____   Location _____

Sides ☐   Headshot ☐   Resume ☐

Pieces Performed

1. _____
2. _____
3. _____

Outfit _____

Behind the Table

Name	Contact Info	Feedback Received

Notes

Feeling 😕 😮 😲 🙂 😃   Call Back? ☐

Production _____   Date _____

Role _____   Time _____

Casting Director _____   Location _____

Sides ☐   Headshot ☐   Resume ☐

Pieces Performed

1. _____
2. _____
3. _____

Outfit _____

Behind the Table

Name	Contact Info	Feedback Received

Notes

Feeling   Call Back? ☐

Production _____   Date _____

Role _____   Time _____

Casting Director _____   Location _____

Sides ☐   Headshot ☐   Resume ☐

Pieces Performed

1. _____
2. _____
3. _____

Outfit _____

Behind the Table

Name	Contact Info	Feedback Received

Notes

Feeling    Call Back? ☐

Production _____   Date _____

Role _____   Time _____

Casting Director _____   Location _____

Sides ☐   Headshot ☐   Resume ☐

Pieces Performed

1. _____
2. _____
3. _____

Outfit _____

Behind the Table

Name	Contact Info	Feedback Received

Notes

Feeling   Call Back? ☐

Production		Date	
Role		Time	
Casting Director		Location	

Sides ☐   Headshot ☐   Resume ☐

Pieces Performed

1. _____
2. _____
3. _____

Outfit _____

Behind the Table

Name	Contact Info	Feedback Received

Notes

Feeling 😐 😮 😯 🙂 😀   Call Back? ☐

Production _____ Date _____

Role _____ Time _____

Casting Director _____ Location _____

Sides ☐   Headshot ☐   Resume ☐

Pieces Performed

1. _____
2. _____
3. _____

Outfit _____

Behind the Table

Name	Contact Info	Feedback Received

Notes

Feeling   Call Back? ☐

Production _____   Date _____

Role _____   Time _____

Casting Director _____   Location _____

Sides ☐   Headshot ☐   Resume ☐

Pieces Performed

1. _____
2. _____
3. _____

Outfit _____

Behind the Table

Name	Contact Info	Feedback Received

Notes

_____
_____
_____
_____

Feeling   Call Back? ☐

Production _____   Date _____

Role _____   Time _____

Casting Director _____   Location _____

Sides ☐   Headshot ☐   Resume ☐

Pieces Performed

1. _____
2. _____
3. _____

Outfit _____

Behind the Table

Name	Contact Info	Feedback Received

Notes

Feeling    Call Back? ☐

Production _____ **Date** _____

Role _____ Time _____

Casting Director _____ Location _____

Sides ☐ Headshot ☐ Resume ☐

Pieces Performed

1. _____
2. _____
3. _____

Outfit _____

Behind the Table

Name	Contact Info	Feedback Received

Notes

Feeling 😐 😮 😲 🙂 😄   Call Back? ☐

Production _____ **Date** _____

Role _____ Time _____

Casting Director _____ Location _____

Sides ☐   Headshot ☐   Resume ☐

Pieces Performed

1. _____
2. _____
3. _____

Outfit _____

Behind the Table

Name	Contact Info	Feedback Received

Notes

_____

Feeling   Call Back? ☐

Production _____   **Date** _____

Role _____   **Time** _____

Casting Director _____   **Location** _____

Sides ☐   Headshot ☐   Resume ☐

Pieces Performed

1. _____
2. _____
3. _____

Outfit _____

Behind the Table

Name	Contact Info	Feedback Received

Notes

Feeling   Call Back? ☐

Production _____   Date _____

Role _____   Time _____

Casting Director _____   Location _____

Sides ☐   Headshot ☐   Resume ☐

Pieces Performed

1. _____
2. _____
3. _____

Outfit _____

Behind the Table

Name	Contact Info	Feedback Received

Notes

Feeling   Call Back? ☐

Production _____   Date _____

Role _____   Time _____

Casting Director _____   Location _____

Sides ☐   Headshot ☐   Resume ☐

Pieces Performed

1. _____
2. _____
3. _____

Outfit _____

Behind the Table

Name	Contact Info	Feedback Received

Notes

Feeling   Call Back? ☐

Production _____   Date _____

Role _____   Time _____

Casting Director _____   Location _____

Sides ☐   Headshot ☐   Resume ☐

Pieces Performed

1. _____
2. _____
3. _____

Outfit _____

Behind the Table

Name	Contact Info	Feedback Received

Notes

Feeling    Call Back? ☐

Production _____	Date _____

Role _____	Time _____

Casting Director _____	Location _____

Sides ☐   Headshot ☐   Resume ☐

Pieces Performed

1. _____
2. _____
3. _____

Outfit _____

Behind the Table

Name	Contact Info	Feedback Received

Notes

Feeling    Call Back? ☐

Production _____ **Date** _____

Role _____ **Time** _____

Casting Director _____ **Location** _____

Sides ☐ Headshot ☐ Resume ☐

Pieces Performed

1. _____
2. _____
3. _____

Outfit _____

Behind the Table

Name	Contact Info	Feedback Received

Notes

Feeling   Call Back? ☐

Production _____   Date _____

Role _____   Time _____

Casting Director _____   Location _____

Sides ☐   Headshot ☐   Resume ☐

Pieces Performed

1. _____
2. _____
3. _____

Outfit _____

Behind the Table

Name	Contact Info	Feedback Received

Notes

_____
_____
_____
_____

Feeling    Call Back? ☐

Production _____ **Date** _____

Role _____ Time _____

Casting Director _____ Location _____

Sides ☐ Headshot ☐ Resume ☐

Pieces Performed

1. _____
2. _____
3. _____

Outfit _____

Behind the Table

Name	Contact Info	Feedback Received

Notes

Feeling   Call Back? ☐

Production _____   Date _____

Role _____   Time _____

Casting Director _____   Location _____

Sides ☐   Headshot ☐   Resume ☐

Pieces Performed

1. _____
2. _____
3. _____

Outfit _____

Behind the Table

Name	Contact Info	Feedback Received

Notes

Feeling    Call Back? ☐

Production _____   Date _____

Role _____   Time _____

Casting Director _____   Location _____

Sides ☐   Headshot ☐   Resume ☐

Pieces Performed

1. _____
2. _____
3. _____

Outfit _____

Behind the Table

Name	Contact Info	Feedback Received

Notes

_____
_____
_____
_____

Feeling   Call Back? ☐

Production _____   Date _____

Role _____   Time _____

Casting Director _____   Location _____

Sides ☐   Headshot ☐   Resume ☐

Pieces Performed

1. _____
2. _____
3. _____

Outfit _____

Behind the Table

Name	Contact Info	Feedback Received

Notes

_____

Feeling   Call Back? ☐

Production _____   Date _____

Role _____   Time _____

Casting Director _____   Location _____

Sides ☐   Headshot ☐   Resume ☐

Pieces Performed

1. _____
2. _____
3. _____

Outfit _____

Behind the Table

Name	Contact Info	Feedback Received

Notes

_____

Feeling   Call Back? ☐

Production _____ **Date** _____

Role _____ Time _____

Casting Director _____ Location _____

Sides ☐   Headshot ☐   Resume ☐

Pieces Performed

1. _____
2. _____
3. _____

Outfit _____

Behind the Table

Name	Contact Info	Feedback Received

Notes

Feeling   Call Back? ☐

Production _____   Date _____

Role _____   Time _____

Casting Director _____   Location _____

Sides ☐   Headshot ☐   Resume ☐

Pieces Performed

1. _____
2. _____
3. _____

Outfit _____

Behind the Table

Name	Contact Info	Feedback Received

Notes

_____
_____
_____
_____

Feeling   Call Back? ☐

Production _____   Date _____

Role _____   Time _____

Casting Director _____   Location _____

Sides ☐   Headshot ☐   Resume ☐

Pieces Performed

1. _____
2. _____
3. _____

Outfit _____

Behind the Table

Name	Contact Info	Feedback Received

Notes

[   ]

Feeling    Call Back? ☐

Production _____   Date _____

Role _____   Time _____

Casting Director _____   Location _____

Sides ☐   Headshot ☐   Resume ☐

Pieces Performed

1. _____
2. _____
3. _____

Outfit _____

Behind the Table

Name	Contact Info	Feedback Received

Notes

Feeling   Call Back? ☐

Production _____ Date _____

Role _____ Time _____

Casting Director _____ Location _____

Sides ☐   Headshot ☐   Resume ☐

Pieces Performed

1. _____
2. _____
3. _____

Outfit _____

Behind the Table

Name	Contact Info	Feedback Received

Notes

Feeling    Call Back? ☐

Production _____   Date _____

Role _____   Time _____

Casting Director _____   Location _____

Sides ☐   Headshot ☐   Resume ☐

Pieces Performed

1. _____
2. _____
3. _____

Outfit _____

Behind the Table

Name	Contact Info	Feedback Received

Notes

Feeling   Call Back? ☐

Production _____   Date _____

Role _____   Time _____

Casting Director _____   Location _____

Sides ☐   Headshot ☐   Resume ☐

Pieces Performed

1. _____
2. _____
3. _____

Outfit _____

Behind the Table

Name	Contact Info	Feedback Received

Notes

_____
_____
_____
_____

Feeling   😃   Call Back? ☐

Production _____ **Date** _____

Role _____ Time _____

Casting Director _____ Location _____

Sides ☐ Headshot ☐ Resume ☐

Pieces Performed

1. _____
2. _____
3. _____

Outfit _____

Behind the Table

Name	Contact Info	Feedback Received

Notes

Feeling   Call Back? ☐

Production _____   Date _____

Role _____   Time _____

Casting Director _____ Location _____

Sides ☐   Headshot ☐   Resume ☐

Pieces Performed

1. _____
2. _____
3. _____

Outfit _____

Behind the Table

Name	Contact Info	Feedback Received

Notes

_____

Feeling   Call Back? ☐

Manufactured by Amazon.ca
Bolton, ON